FIRST   12149
EDITION $12.88

D1526557

Anna
and the
Steel Mill

Anna
and the

Steel Mill

Deborah Burnham

Texas Tech University Press

Copyright 1995 Texas Tech University Press

All rights reserved. No portion of this book may be reproduced in
any form or by any means, including electronic storage and retrieval
systems, except by explicit, prior written permission of the publisher
except for brief passages excerpted for review and critical purposes.

This book was set in Caslon and printed on acid-free paper that meets
the Giudelines for permanence and durability of the Committee on
Production Giudelines for Book Longevity of the Council on Library
Resources.

Printed in the United States of America

Jacket design by Kerri Carter

Cover and frontis photo from the Jones and Laughlin Steel company
Records, reprinted courtesy of Library and Archives Division,
Historical Society of Western Pennsylvania, Pittsburgh, PA.

Library of Congress Cataloging-in-Publication Data
Burnham, Deborah
    Anna and the steel mill / Deborah Burnham.
      p.   cm.
    ISBN 0-89672-345-3 (alk. paper)
    1. Italian American families—Ohio—Poetry. 2. Italian
Americans—Ohio—Poetry. 3. Family—Ohio—Poetry. I. Title.
PS3552.U7323A83 1995
811'.54—dc20   94-31356
                                                     CIP

95 96 97 98 99 00 01 02 03 / 9 8 7 6 5 4 3 2 1

Texas Tech University Press
P. O. Box 41037
Lubbock, Texas 79409-1037 USA
1-800-832-4042

Acknowledgments

These poems, several in earlier versions, first appeared in the following publications, to whom grateful acknowledgment is made:

Beloit Poetry Journal: "School Fire"
Graham House Review: "The Loudest Woman in Lake Erie"
Kansas Quarterly: "The Fishery: Cleaning"
Poetry: "When the Unimaginable Becomes Easy" and "Forgetting"
Poetry Northwest: "Climbing the Trestle" (published as "Walking the Trestle")
Virginia Quarterly Review: "Making Sure of Arithmetic: Grades 1–6"
West Branch: "Born of Water and the Spirit," "Fire in the Onion Field," "Perfect Game," "Praising Their Names: The Market, Lewisburg, Pennsylvania," and "The Stolen Child"

Much of this book was written in time made available by a grant from the National Endowment for the Arts.

I would like to thank Darcy Cummings, Jeanne Walker, and The Philadelphia Women Writers.

To my family

Foreword

It is a pleasure to read a new poet with an individual voice and her own way of looking slantwise at experience. Deborah Burnham's poems begin in memories, her own or those of persons she has imagined; these are transformed into other, richer realizations than the acts or thoughts that brought them into being. A poem on memory—it is titled "Forgetting"—lists several things she can't remember, moving toward this resolution:

> I'm trying to recall the story of the Baal
> Shem Tov who forgot his life's accumulation—
> tales, laws, history—all but the letter K.
> Tending that small seed, he found his world again.
> I sing myself to sleep with ABC and cling
> to the useful letters that spell *milk* and *kiss*
> knowing they'll feed me when there is nothing else.

Fortunately, there is much else. The venue of many of her poems is her native Ohio; of others, Philadelphia, where she now lives. Her Ohio poems range in time across two centuries. One set brings us an Italian family emigrating to Cleveland after the second world war, and dramatizes their acculturation. In another group the settlers are nineteenth-century pioneers, a shipwreck of Irish and German emigrants, proprieters of the underground railroad, a visionary. Still other poems draw on her own life, as in one that commences with grade-school arithmetic problems demonstrated by her father, until his illness changes the terms of the problem to

> let n
> be any man's capacity for pain—
> a deep tank with a dime-sized leak and a thick
> efficient hose that runs all night; n + 1
> will fill it, overflowing

Ms. Burnham's poems get inside the minds of, and empathize with, her characters, be they laid-off workers in a steel mill, Amish farmers, a crazed tenant who blockades his flat with piled newspapers, herself as a child, or her own child. A half-demented street man warns construction workers that sunlight reflected from their glass tower could destroy the city; their shift over, they find him sleeping, and "circle him with plastic / safety cones" and shield his eyes "from the orange sodium glare of streetlights / burning like the city's anger." The life of a fishery worker is infested by "a stink of fish" that gets into her pastry dough, taints her laundry; yet even this oppressive work carries its own redemption, as a fishscale stuck to her wrist "fell to her child's pillow / like a jewel as she bent to say goodnight." These poems, transcending affliction and suffering, define their speaker's generosity of feeling.

Ms. Burnham has confidence in the power of metaphor, whether in the action described or in the words by which they are defined. One of her poems enriched by both symbolic action and associative diction is "Born of Water and the Spirit":

> The Baptist preacher's daughter showed me the huge
> tank her father scrubbed each time the faithful
> washed away old lives of flesh and sin.
> They wear white robes and socks, Jane told me; water
> must touch every inch of skin—even
> her father's fingers on an arm would give sin
> a hiding place to grow, like mold under wet hay.
> My church taught that sin is bodiless,
> invisible until clothed in word or deed,
> but I knew sin is like the fine lake sand,
> hiding in the soft folds between my legs.
> The Baptist's cleansing pool was cold and still;
> I knew that to wash sin away, water
> must pull you down and under until you cry,
> opening your whole body to the undertow
> that coils like muscle underneath the foam.

These lines skillfully embody the dialectics between rival theologies, between sin and purification each embodied physically, between the pastoral suggestion of "mold under wet hay" and the oceanic image of "undertow." The implied sexuality of the final lines is projected into the undefined "lives of flesh and sin" undergoing immersion in the opening lines.

Deborah Burnham writes with assurance and quiet authority. From among many poems, I choose this one to exemplify her subtle delineation of the search for transcendence and the relationship, the possible confusion, of revelation and illusion:

Following the Prophet

When the Mormon prophet came to Kirtland,
he brought words of fire and gold that lured young
Peter from the Methodists to the river,
where he paced the bank and watched for something
shining through the golden aspens. Once he saw
an angel, black as a starless night,
holding a scrap of white that Peter knew
to be a letter sent from Heaven
to Ohio. He called; the angel's
midnight wings glowed upon the river's
face; he waded out to catch the letter
that would tell him where in all Ohio
he could feel his soul glow golden
as the aspens, all year long. He watched
the angel graze the treetops, blue-black
as a grackle, while the message caught
like a wet leaf at the river's distant
edge and sank in the swift water.

The economy of means in these two poems is characteristic of the rest; no detail is extraneous, each contributes to the emergence of theme and feeling. The way is opened to complex responses in language accessible as ordinary speech, intensified by the design of the poems. A first book showing such skill, such range, is indeed a joyful event, and a harbinger of compelling work to come.

Daniel Hoffman

Contents

West to Ohio

City Life

Anna
and the
Steel Mill

West to Ohio: 1950

We were leaving Naples about five or six o'clock, approximately dusk time, and as we left I could see on my left the Vesuvius—and that stood out so vividly with big smoke coming out ... At night you could see the flames of the mountain.

Frank Santoni
Island of Hope, Island of Tears

Anna Leaving Home

(Italy to Ohio: 1950)

Giuseppe had been restless since their wedding;
Anna knew he thought about Ohio
and his brother who sowed and weeded there
at the best nursery. He had a Ford,
Giuseppe told her, while she cleared the oily
plates; don't worry, I'll make money and you
can learn to drive. Anna had read those letters
from Ohio; Eduardo told them how
the rose fields looked—gold shading into pearl,
bursts of scarlet, then the dark treeline,
then the lake wind, blowing sand into the trees.
His wife Camille picked pebbles from her garden,
wondered what grew best in sand, and wondered
why she'd come so far to get the only patch
of bad earth in the county.

                      Anna washed the plates
and held them on her lap until they dried.
How could she make bread where food is wrapped
in squares? The oil, she heard, is made from corn.
Would she practice in that car, then drive east
across Ohio to the ocean, facing
Europe and park on the blowing sand? The gulls
and terns would laugh, but not, at least, in English.

3

Getting on the Ark

God promised Noah he wouldn't flood the earth again,
but some say he never promised not to burn us.
While their village dried and crackled in the unrelenting
sun, Anna and Giuseppe sailed from Naples,
feeling the salt air like a damp blessing,
feeling seven years of dust sift from their skins,
fleeing their land of dust and rock, and wind
that turns the rock to dust, covering trees
and gardens, deadly as a flood. The boat
was jammed with tanners, carters, harvesters of grapes
and olives, priests and madmen, as if God had told the harried
captain to fill the berths with every human sort
to save them all from choking on the dust they could neither
breathe nor eat. Only the barbers, priests, and madmen
still had work; the dry wind had blown the rest away.

Basil and Anna

Coming to Ohio was like exile;
in Italy, her green and purple basil
grew past her knees, and when she picked the last
before the frost, it stained her fingers brown
as if she'd smoked the cigarettes her father
and her brothers and her uncles rolled, lounging
on the stone steps, worn by three centuries
of men who gathered after dinner. Once
she tried to smoke burnt ends and a bit
of basil; she choked, and her uncles laughed.

When her restless husband took her to Ohio,
she stood outside the supermarket, staring
at the trucks of food hidden in brown boxes,
at the faces—cream blond Finns, Hungarians
tanned darker than her shoe, the others
whose name, *niro*, she knew from home.
They stared at her; she wanted to rub her face
with basil, like the restless princess
who darkened her fair skin with walnut juice
and walked unnoticed through strange kingdoms.
Anna walked past Woolworth's, practiced English
reading labels, passed the bakery where all the crusts
were soft, to the river where spring floods soaked
the baseball fields. She filled cans with that rich dirt
to make a garden for her basil's crumpled leaves,
rough and acrid as the sounds of English.
Crushed, they bloomed with the smell of sun; she kept
    them
through the winter in jars of salt and oil, believing
like everyone at home, that basil, sharp
as it is, could wake the sweet milk sleeping
in a woman's breasts.

Anna at Euclid Beach

That first week in America, "Giuseppe"
turned to "Joe," Anna snipped "Maria"
from her name, and Joe's brother drove them all
to the amusement park. They wondered
at the saint whose feast day spawned a carnival
that filled the beach. Eddy laughed; "It's built here—
it's open every summer" and loaded
Joe and Anna on the ferris wheel. They rode
up, claiming the lake, green that day, and always
dangerous, claiming the lake freighter full of cars,
claiming the great stone houses ringing Cleveland,
then losing their new fortunes in the hazardous
downward swoop with a dime left for one more ride.
Camille and Anna rode the Centrifuge,
pressing their backs against the leather padding,
soft as the back seat of a car, feeling
their stomachs dip as the round room began
to whirl and the floor dropped from beneath their feet.
They stuck to the soft walls—a miracle!
Anna hadn't heard such screaming since the war,
when no one ever screamed except in terror,
or when the news came that Giovanni, the only
boy from that unhealthy village who was deemed
fit enough to die in combat, had been shot.
But Camille was laughing, hiccuping; later
she told Anna it was like the first time
with Eddy in the back seat of Caranci's
Chevrolet, lying down so willingly,
held by his slight weight, his damp hair, his panting,
the bottom dropping out around her
and she could barely raise her head, or sigh.

6

First Swim

Sundays, they went to early Mass, then drove
to Fairport Beach where, two thousand years ago,
the lighthouse hill and Diamond Alkali's
sulfurous fields were covered by the ancient lake.
It dried up, leaving soil rich enough
for the roses whose peach and gold and crimson
made Anna blink; she would have liked to pace
their fragrant aisles, instead of swimming—
she hadn't seen her thighs in sunlight
since the war. Camille tied Anna's borrowed suit,
showed her how to stretch out on the Army blanket
and lit her a cigarette. The sun flashed;
Anna could have been back home, in the olive
orchards, but here, after burying the stump
of cigarette, she was doing nothing—
not knitting, not picking gravel from a pan
of beans, just lying, as if she were a rose
whose job it was to lean into the sun.
She started to explain this: Camille said
"Turn over now," in English.

All summer, Anna heard the church bells, muffled
in the damp air as if the ancient lake
had risen past the steeples. All summer,
she refused to swim; she'd heard the lake
grew weeds to loop her ankles and drag her
to its cold green heart. Water would pull her
and the beach, the lighthouse hill, the rose fields
into itself again. Camille coaxed her out;
she stood, knee-deep, soothed by the lapping waves,
while children swam in circles around her legs,
bobbing up amazed, as if they saw the sand
and clouds for the first time, as if they took

their first mouthful of dry air. The smallest
choked and flailed; Anna carried him to shore,
made him breathe and cry, swaddled him in towels,
seeing as she held him the sharp black shadow
of a gull, moving over sand and water
like a blessing or a slow announcement.

Learning to Read

In America, everything had names; writing
filled the air like gnats, and made Anna's eyes itch.
She longed to read, not just *coffee, bread,* and *rose,*
but the thorny names that filled the birth and death page
of the *Telegraph.* She spelled them to Camille
who spoke them, then made her say each one three times,
as once she'd practiced a and b and c.
She spelled Hakola, Laakso, Kallio; the Finnish
names breathed their fluid vowels. She read a headline:
Diamond Alkali Plans Layoffs and thought it was a wealthy
Finnish woman. Camille snorted—the Finns just work there,
and no one knows who owns it. One day, to test herself,
Anna read the phone book, a quarter inch of close-packed
names and at the end sang Zapitelli, Franco,
Zapitelli, Joseph, Zapitelli, Salvatore!

Now she could read the funnies! She followed
Dondi, shipped from Italy on an airplane
full of baffled orphans, his greenhorn cap
sagging on his shaggy hair. She knew
his short life before she read it: how long
his mother coughed, how she missed the GI
father, dead before he knew he had a son.
Each day, Anna followed Dondi off to school,
heard the school yard yelling *wop* and *guinea,*
learning what they meant. She thought she knew,
more than his awkward second father, how to bring
a foreign child into this strange green world, full
of thorny names, and snow, and roses
that the growers name for things they cannot buy:
Forever Young, Peace, Chrysler Imperial.

Queen for a Day

When the Carancis got the block's first
television, they invited two each day
to gaze at the six-inch screen. Camille
chose "Queen for a Day", and explained to Anna
how the silver needle measured the applause
for One and Two and Three, straining from sadness
into suffering, while Marie, the elfin
helper, pulled the veils from washer-dryers,
stoves, and televisions. As the winner
wept into her roses, pulled the fur across
her housedress, Anna wondered how the silver
needle would behave in her village square.
What if everyone who gave a son
to Mussolini wept into the microphone?
What about the whispered tales of Silvia
who was shot and tumbled into a dusty
hole? Some say she resisted first one soldier,
then another; some say she smuggled
cheese and money under her wide skirts. But
who would dare tell her story, since just
her name, breathed into the dust, could bring
a torch or bullet through the window?
Would the dry hills echo with applause,
blowing dust from unburied bones? But after
the drought that lasted longer than the war,
who is left to clap?

At the Zoo

Pausing by the thick iron cages, Anna wondered
how the elephants and lions came
to Cleveland, and how they stood the winter.
Joe, Camille and Eddy chattered on
in English; Anna caught their boss's name,
heard *truck* and *rosebush;* she whispered "Too much
English," but their talk just mocked her silence.
So she watched the chimps who chuffed and grunted,
ignoring her as if they too were speaking
English. She remembered deaf, mad Bruna,
who gave new names to those who refused her
bread and cheese. Once, the tavern owner threw
a loaf at her; she'd been crooning names
she'd given him, that rhymed with words for *stingy,*
pig, and *cuckold.* After that, the wives left
food for her, wrapped up in rags, and after dark.
They never said her name, hoping she'd
forget to whisper names she'd given them,
hoping if she ate, she wouldn't talk, or sing.

Anna watched giraffes and lions, asking them
if they'd forgotten how to greet the huge
dawn over the grasslands. She named a hundred
beasts, not in English or Italian, but
in gutturals that sounded like dry grasses,
like wind hot enough to blow their scent away
from captors, like their racing feet.

Anna and the Steel Mill

Riding home from Cleveland, Anna watched the steel mill
lift its red fists, scorching the damp night. She knew about
the mill; their neighbor sweated there, watching the wet steel
swing itself from vat to mold. She knew if she could work
there, heat would pare her body to a man's bone and sinew.
She'd grow strong enough to sail a small boat back to Italy.

Her aunt once explained the world to her, to keep her home:
the sea breaks off and falls, ships slide like saucers
from the table. But she'd be strong enough to hold
the sails taut as her boat tacked around the dragons
guarding the hungry margins of the earth.
She could watch fire exploding from their mouths, enough
to heat the midnight ocean and char the sails,
just as the foundry man, unblinking, watches the steel flare,
spill, tossing sparks as big as plums against his leather vest.

Playing Catch

One night, their neighbor found old gloves, took Joe
and Anna to the school yard to teach them
baseball—two greenhorns and a hometown girl
laughing as the ball hopped, Joe's white T-shirt
glimmering in the dusk, Anna's dark dress
invisible. She showed them how to grip
a wash rag and practice at the bathroom
mirror, how to fire pebbles at the maple tree.
Anna wondered if the girl would pitch
and slide when she got married, but, too shy
to ask, she grabbed a spotted apple,
put her arm back and fired, straight at the waiting tree.

Joe started playing every night with Eddy,
after the World Series, after the first
frost, when they spent all day tying roses
up with burlap against winter. They pitched
and caught, pretending they each stood with eight
men on perfect grass, in June. They called out
teams, one always from New York, the other
all Italian: three DiMaggios, Berra
and Rizzuto stolen from the Yankees,
then Francona, Colavito, Garagiola.
Joe wanted Campanella; the name
made him think of bells and fields. Eddy balked;
"He's colored, and we got two catchers."

July: Hail

Until the hailstorm, Anna hadn't seen
the rose fields; they were wide enough to hold
four villages, with room for a hundred
exiles at the damp edges. She lost count
of the broken blooms, thinking how the altars
dripped with roses when the Monsignor died.
When Eddy whispered they should take all
they could carry, they heaped the backseat
with scarred and sandy buds, and the sharp smell
of rain. Anna took cuttings from a smashed bush—
no leaves, just the shiny thorns. Eddy told her
how to keep them in wet sand, until the roots
come, naked as worms, then set them
in the garden. He'd slipped into the office,
copied out directions from the grower's book
of secrets: how to make the half-dead
rise and multiply.

First Harvest

Since Christmas, snow had choked the ground in a seamless
blind abundance, then thawed and teased, then fell again,
burying Anna's pear tree past the first branching.
She watched the April sun release the limbs,
like bony women tossing their arms, praying for sun.
She heard the radio say frost might shrivel blossoms
foolish enough to trust a few warm days; she heard the priest
name apples, pears, and cherries for special blessing lest
leaves be the only crop that year. She thought prayer
changed anything but weather; she wanted pears
that autumn with strong cheese and wine.
So she took a bedsheet, wrapped buds and branches
against the freezing air, tied the edges until
it looked like a single mammoth blossom, strong enough
for any weather. She tried to recollect the taste of pears,
and remembered how her aunt would say
don't let the landlord know how good pears taste with cheese—
he'll tax you for them. Her uncle argued; don't let
the peasant know—he'll steal the pears. All summer,
she counted small green pears, then in September
heaped straw under the branches so they could fall,
warm and without a bruise.

Waiting for the Bomb

Their neighbor laughed about the air raid drills at school;
the tiny siren, whining through the sweaty hallways,
boys kneeling on the north side, girls on the south,
fingers knotted on their bent necks as if those fragile
nets of bone and skin could save them from the blades
of glass that, in their sudden freedom, long to test
their edges against something soft.

Anna thought of the only time she'd seen the Germans
take a suspect from her village—a spy, or worse,
they said. He stumbled from his hut, shirt peeling
from his back like a Party poster on the church wall,
hands behind his neck in the universal sign
that says surrender, fingers powerless
to protect his head from blows, shaking like the straw
bars of a cage that holds the smallest birds, the larks
and warblers that the wealthy love to eat.

Walking to Canada

That year, the lake froze solid, shore to shore.
The Caranci kids had planned it out; wool
socks, thermoses of coffee, make ten miles
per hour and land in Canada that night.
They thought they'd slide across the ice as swiftly
as they speed across the skating pond,
the wind propelling them across a perfect
glaze to the town lights of the northern shore.
But the waves had frozen up in humps
with no clear path, as if a white field of wolves
lay sleeping there, and might wake to scream.

Their parents found them shivering on the sand,
no hope of telling the whole school how they'd
dared the gray, unmoved, unmoving lake.
Their mother laughed at the bits of food they'd packed—
they must have hoped their bread and cheese would stretch
across the solid miles to Canada,
or that willing fish would razor through
the ice and leap into their hands.

Anna marveled—they could go from one
country to another without papers,
without the fear of guns or uniforms
she'd carried when she left her village.
When she left Italy, she'd folded up
her heart so carefully it couldn't see
the silvery dry hills, couldn't see the dark
waves rising like muscles on the mason's
back as he lifts stones that are loath to move.
The water heaved the packed ship toward America,
all the time her heart protesting as if
the journey were on foot, shoeless, over jagged ice.

The Lake, the Town,
the Gardens

Bandstand

It's 1958, and I know nothing that I really want
to know. It's four o'clock; our TV screen, smaller
than a dinner plate, leaps with pageboys, crew cuts,
   and white shirts.
My baby sister wears a clean white cast from her tiny
nipples to her toes; she'll be just fine, my parents say,
when her hip has grown a proper socket around the bone,
she'll jitterbug and ride a bike, you'll see! I kiss
her damp neck and cheeks, testing her against the smiling
children just diagnosed with cancer that the Cleveland
paper shows us every week or so. She tries to wiggle,
laughing at the music, lying on her stomach
like a stiff white frog, while kids in Philadelphia
teach the Midwest how to dance away from awkwardness.
All I didn't know flickered on that screen; Dick Clark,
who would not grow old, the city's windows, silvered
by the western sun, tight jeans and blouses,
dancing—those mortal messages washed about me
like rain on asphalt. While some boy sang about his baby,
I'd bounce my sister in her plaster jacket, loving her
as I loved nothing else. "She's my baby, all the time"
I sang to the tune of "Jesus Loves Me"; the clean pale skins
agreed, dancing through the endless afternoon.

Making Sure of Arithmetic:
Grades 1-6

Story problems were the worst; how many
quarts per hour flow through a tank
of X capacity and a slow leak? How long
will Paul and Jane, driving at constant speeds
in mismatched cars, stay in Ohio? I'd fuss
and whine; my patient father sketched out tanks
with drains, and one night made a siphon
with a rubber hose, drawing a sink of water
down into the tub to show how water
can travel by itself. He graphed its speed;
his voice flowed across my stubborn mind
as relentless as the lake that fills
itself and flows out through a thousand leaks
while the world's water multiplies itself,
just like the errors in my father's blood
that sent him to the Clinic while we wrote
new problems for ourselves, not Jane and Paul.
How often can you see him if each time
it costs you fifty miles, and one pure lie
repeated X times: it's better, better.
Let X be the cup of soup and Y the bread
you coax down his blistered throat; how many
loaves will rot in him before his flesh says no?
The lake will freeze by Christmas, but the bread,
the miles, the lie will keep on running; let n
be any man's capacity for pain—
a deep tank with a dime-sized leak and a thick
efficient hose that runs all night; n + 1
will fill it, overflowing.

Forgetting

It's the third act of *Three Sisters;* Masha's weeping
at the window; she's forgotten the Italian word
for "bird," they'll never leave that village, snow has turned
to rain, and with each freeze and thaw she'll lose a few
more foreign words that once she'd hoped to use in Moscow,
flirting. I've forgotten all Ohio's counties,
and the last verse of "A Mighty Fortress" after
"let goods and kindred go." I've lost the clever linkage
of Dickinson and Mick Jagger that I've used
to woo my classes. Is there, under my lame tongue,
a word that means the milk-sweet smell of my child's hair
from those first days when we thought we'd remember
everything? A word that brings the plunge of blood from head
to groin during that first kiss? Is it enough to know
that they existed, holding the empty word
like a vial whose perfume has dried up?
Anyway, it was Irina, not her sister,
weeping; it was the words for "ceiling" and for "window"
she'd forgotten, though in time she'd lose them all.
I'm trying to recall the story of the Baal
Shem Tov who forgot his life's accumulation—
tales, laws, history—all but the letter K.
Tending that small seed, he found his world again.
I sing myself to sleep with ABC and cling
to the useful letters that spell *milk* and *kiss*
knowing they'll feed me when there is nothing else.

The Princess and the Pea

When we were told the story of the princess
whose delicacy was tested by the pea
under the forty mattresses and feather beds;
when we were told how cramped and bruised she was
after a single night, half the second grade
was skeptical, claiming mattresses could pad
a cannonball, and the rest were silent,
wanting to believe.
They'd grow up thinking that the stones of grief
and anger piled under our limp pillows
only bruise the royal, and leave the rest
of us like horses who must sleep
on cobbles, who must somehow feel loss and wonder
but who don't display their bruises, or complain.

The Stolen Child

When she didn't come to lunch or supper,
rumors grew fat and loud: a trucker stole her,
a freed thief, a gypsy. Such slander thrilled me:
I'd seen their fires and battered trucks
beside the water, heard they stole pears, laundry, dogs.

When they found her bones, I wondered if she looked
like bones we found behind the shed, birds and cats
smeared with leaves, spilled like jackstraws.
We'd rinse skull and ribs, fit spines together
then lay them out as if they'd gone to sleep.

Cleaning Chicken

Growing up, I cleaned a thousand
chickens at the sink, tearing wads
of fat bright as marigolds
from the neckhole, squeezing
black clots from the heart that seemed
too small to pump life through the bulk
of breast and thigh, and, like our hearts,
too narrow to conduct the flow
of terror at the shadow
of a whistling hawk. I'd scrape
the slick clots down the sink's steel throat,
losing any chance to get
the wisdom running through the blood
and stored in its straining heart.
We ate the chicken which I'd stripped
of grief, surprise and terror,
wondering where in our muddled
bodies all our wisdom hides
and, short of squeezing our limp
hearts, how we could get it back.

Ocean City

fills with Methodists in summertime. Their hymns
at breakfast scrub and sanctify the air,
so they weren't surprised to see, one day
on the broad beach, an Amish family, their blue
and violet shirts glowing like hydrangeas
amid the salty, oiled skins. After the first
stares, no one paid them mind; the sea's the largest
miracle we have, and why should everyone
not want to see it? They found scraps of shell
which glowed inside their pockets, reminding them
that soon they'd bend into the green and yellow
fields they'd sown, heaping corn and squash in baskets
like Peter, Andrew, James and John who plucked
fish from the sea's ripe garden. They set
their boots and sneakers in neat rows and stepped
into the ocean, shy at first, but soon trusting
the smooth waves. They sang while cold salt water
rinsed the stains of weariness from their clothes
and hands, rejoicing as the water held them
up, off their tired feet. The oldest woman
floated past them, feeling the water ease
her life of weeding corn and scrubbing walls.
She felt her skirts grow heavy as the woolen
blankets she'd wrung out for sixty years;
she floated farther and began to sink,
pulled by the weight of tasks she could not finish,
her pockets full of clicking shells.

Fire in the Onion Field

The soil in those fields is so
rich it can catch fire. Blazing
black dirt isn't easily controlled.
John McPhee

The mole never sees the sun that warms his wiggling
fur through earth so rich it burns when a loose
spark lands in a furrow. The fire that summer
scorched a million onions lying in dry
cracks deep enough to hide a man. The fire
leaped gaps, rejoicing at the air then dove
into the earth, warming onions so the green
fingers at their cores began to steam.
Their perfume spread in smoke to a mole's nose
who felt the heat as if a stray sun
had exploded in the field and lay there,
puffing fire. His throat, soft as an eyelid,
swelled, and he tore an onion's crackling paper,
longing for its water. Fire bubbled through
his eyes; he clung to a hot root while his fur
curled and browned like elm leaves in September.
His paws fluttered as he swam across the sun.

Praising Their Names: The Market, Lewisburg, Pennsylvania

Praise Sarah Yoder, Ebenezer Stoltz,
a score of Zooks, a hundred Abrahams.
Praise apples they pick at dawn, then haul in split pecks
the tiny greens, mild goldens large as a digger's fist.
Weeks named by apples ripening from July's astringent greens—
praise Transparent, Lodi, Rambo—
to September reds—Cortland, McIntosh, Jonathan with scarlet
    veins,
the late Grimes Golden, bright as zinnias, yielding to a spoon.
Praise russets that went wild, then disappeared.

Praise cucumbers: warts and soft seeds, thick as a miller's
    thumb.
Praise them while the last frost lingers in the pickling crocks.
Praise zucchini, big as boots, that multiply like gnats:
six for every child, cat, pig and robin in the county.

Praise pears that lie like pebbles
in the first stomach of the greedy calf.

Praise the crackling of onion skin, the white's whisper.
It repeats the sun's words: sulfur, burning sugar, tears.

Praise Christ Lapp whose hands swing a side of pig.
Praise Rachel whose hands are rich with sage and bay
    she pounds in sausage.
Praise their cows who, despairing, rubbed bald spots

on their backs, jostling the planks that penned them in the
    truck,
banging their horns and wailing before the blade.

Praise Martha Zimmerman and Daniel who rose at three to
    bake,
whose loaves could make a tower to the sky so light and sweet
angels would swoop around it, forgetting anthems,
praising only yeast.

Roadside Stand

That summer, seven farmers hired a jobless man
to watch their stand since the old way—leave your money
in a basket—wasn't working. He painted signs
with berries big as cabbages, and when the corn
came in, he showed up in a corn suit his wife had stitched
from Woolworth's remnants—yellow from the ankles up,
then a jagged green cape and a tasseled cap.
Cars slowed down to look, then left with four dozen ears.
Once, a van drove up, from the camp in Cleveland where sick
     kids—
some thin, some puffy, all balding—stayed. He unzipped
his suit for them, showed them how his corn silk was
     stitched
into his cap, how, underneath the yarn and cotton,
he was bald. They rubbed his bare skull for luck; he gave
each one an ear for dinner. Two girls husked theirs
and laid the squeaking silk across each other's head
because it was cool and smelled like rain,
because it matched the pale fuzz just coming back.

Climbing the Trestle

If you stand there in the morning when the first train
shakes rust from the loose bolts, you'll hear
    the road crew grumbling
the bridge is cursed, the bridge will fall because the builders
never fed the spirit who demands a price
for anything built near his water. If a gray demon's
sulking in this marsh, he wants the girl
who climbed the bridge last winter to jump, rather than
confess. She came down when her father, his lips and hands
graying in the cold lake wind, promised he wouldn't ask her
why. She went to Cleveland anyway, left
her baby with the gray nuns and came back
to find her story spreading like the fine grit
that sifts down from the tracks.

When the slow train screams at the dawn, the town's women
feel their bodies shaking as if they're sprawling on those cold
tracks, hands knotted, hearing stones plunge into the marsh,
calling their mothers' names, their aunts, listening
for a train. What shakes those tracks, train or sullen spirit,
scares the flash of blue, the heron nesting by the lake
who flies inland before a storm. His wings could heal
the split sky, his great back could lift those women
from their weak perch, set them near the river
where they could wash their faces,
wake up slowly in the sun.

Born of Water and the Spirit

The Baptist preacher's daughter showed me the huge
tank her father scrubbed each time the faithful
washed away old lives of flesh and sin.
They wear white robes and socks, Jane told me; water
must touch every inch of skin—even
her father's fingers on an arm would give sin
a hiding place to grow, like mold under wet hay.
My church taught that sin is bodiless,
invisible until clothed in word or deed,
but I knew sin is like the fine lake sand,
hiding in the soft folds between my legs.
 The Baptist's cleansing pool was cold and still;
 I knew that to wash sin away, water
must pull you down and under until you cry,
opening your whole body to the undertow
that coils like muscle underneath the foam.

Church Camp, 1963

Amos, changed by God from herdsman into
prophet, was our rough hero; he cursed
the worldly Israelites with a fury
we'd never heard from our thoughtful pulpits.
We were virginal, fifteen, and wanted
love far more than an end to poverty,
and so I stared at John, the student
organist, all through "God of Grace
and God of Glory,"—easy, since we all knew
all the words. He showed me how, before he played,
he stretched his hands in a slow tense fist,
shaping tendon around bone to spell
the rapid syllables of Bach's prayers.
 All through grace and vespers I watched him play,
forgetting Amos's strict anger flaring
in the desert without love or music.
I flexed my fingers, as if the tension
puddling in my ignorant body
might gather in my hands, making them
fit instruments of His will, though for prayer
or love or battle, I had no idea.

The First Jet Trail in Painesville

She was eighty and had seen the smoky breath
of engines chase the county's horses
from the roads. She'd learned the dense calligraphy
of clouds: knew storms could crack the fishing boats
and spill the catch. But when the jet trail
wrote its name above the maples, it seemed
as secret as the chalk lines on the blackboard
before she'd learned to read.

When she was eight, she heard of Daniel's wisdom—
how, when Belshazzar, full of lamb and wine,
saw fingers tracing letters on his blank plaster,
he summoned Daniel who spelled out their meaning:

> Your kingdom's days are numbered;
> You have been weighed, found wanting;
> Your land will be divided by the sword.

Who in that town could read the message
in the airplane's smoke before it scattered
in the winds aloft? Who could warn the fishermen
to beware of beasts riding thunderstorms
across the shallow lake, so quick to anger?
Who could warn the farmer of the hailstorm's
early harvest that bruises pears, strips
rosebuds open, all this before the river's
muddy sword cuts the land in two?

The Fishery: Cleaning

Winches scream, silver tons clog the chute;
the day's catch streams from the tarred nets. Perch, pike
flash blue and amber, the only jewels
this gray lake can grow. They spill into the tank;
she grabs two a minute, fish in left hand,
blade in right, head off, tail off, scales flying
in a mica shower against her rubber apron.
Near the channel, a stink of fish hangs
on the cottonwoods, the cooling sand
and in her hair. The stink trails her;
she could quit the fish house, mix dough at midnight
for the baker, but the town would taste catfish
in the pastry, pickerel in the bland
Communion loaf. If she bleached linen
at the hospital, the dying would smell fish
and think the lake had come to carry them
away. Three baths a day can't clean the blood
and oil from her skin. Scales stick to her wrists
and last night, one fell to her child's pillow
like a jewel when she bent to say good night.

Laid Off

The daily *Telegraph* did not explain it, so when
I read that Maria's father, and Mr. Kallio
and Mr. Maki had been laid off by the chemical plant,
I thought of plates and cups, of some large hand
that placed them in a cupboard, toward the back.

The paper didn't say a dozen of them gathered
in the lot after their shift and kicked a black steel
lunch box like a football, back and forth, against the wet
wind from the lake, *clank, clank,* like a press that stamps out
useful things—shoes, or bread, or money, or a clear
bright reason they could take home like a check.
It banged across the lot, closer to the pond
where extra chemicals were dumped—thick, green and yellow,
stinking even in December. The biggest one—
they called him Groza, like the Brown's kicker who could lift
a football between the posts as easily as walking—
sank the lunch box in the pond and the thick green rippled
to the crusted banks. They cheered; he grabbed the rattling
thermos and threw it toward the pond like the last pass
of the last game when they're down by half a dozen
touchdowns and all that matters is the arc it makes,
sailing toward its target, and the dull splash.
It was his heart he threw: full of coffee he was saving
for the cold ride home, full of shivered glass, enough
to cut a factory full of men, the stubborn,
bent and rusted steel around it all.

October 13, 1960

The Pirates and Yankees were tied, three games to
three. The seventh would decide the world champions.

Ike grinned, Jack grinned, lawns east of Cleveland said
   "Keep the Pope
in Italy"; in Hamburg, the short-haired Beatles
practiced "Cry for a Shadow", and we sprawled across
Priscilla's pale blue bedspread, trying to do our
algebra while the score was tied. We knew the Pirates
were the thrifty ones; the Yankees, wasteful as all
city people were, were showing off with twelve
or sixteen runs when four would do. Priscilla's mother
made the bedspread—thirty cents a yard at Woolworth's,
and she had to piece the ruffles, a feat the Yankees
wouldn't understand, though they knew pain. Lou Gehrig
died before Pearl Harbor, and just that day they'd blown
a lead when a hard grounder hit Kubek in the neck.
We thought we heard him groaning through the tiny
radio, and dragged the spread across our knees
because Ohio pulls October snow across
the lake, because Cleveland had finished third that year
in spite of Piersall, Held, Romano, Power,
Bell, Francona; because we didn't know the Beatles
would someday keep us warm by telling us
how cold it would be waiting to grow up.
The score was tied when Mazeroski, the Pirate's
quiet star, stepped up. He could hear all through Ohio
people cheering out their hatred for the Yankees,

so he sent a fastball sailing over fences,
seats and yearning hands, into the smoky sky,
blazing hot and empty as a comet, a false
star that once signaled war and pestilence but now
just swings wide and slow as the Monongahela,
curving back upon the earth, fading,
reminding us how cold it is to wait.

Perfect Game

She needed a ride to Boston; he was driving;
she brought a clutch of tapes against the time when talk
would falter, since they'd never met and had not a thing
in common but their green age and an Ohio friend.
Shy, she asked him for some music, hoping that
the perfect whorls and echoes of the Bach she'd brought
would make trees and vines spring up along the road,
masking asphalt, making talk so easy
 it would seem like singing. Shy, he told her that a tape
was stuck inside the player, but if she didn't mind—
so it happened that they replayed Lenny Barker's
perfect game, May 15, 1981,
against the Blue Jays when the Indians and all
Ohio watched their pitcher set down twenty-seven
batters in a row—four flies, eleven strikeouts,
with a fast ball forty miles per hour faster
than the highway limit. They listened to the small crowd
in their damp seats sigh, then flare with awe and joy
as Bosetti, Woods and Whitt came up, then down
in the ninth, one hundred and three pitches
spent that night; they played the tape again through Newark
past New York, looking through the smoking landscape
for Ohio's sky, which must have glistened, looking
for the lake which must have given birth to a thousand
perfect bass and perch right where the ball park shines
into the water. They said good-bye in Boston,
each seeking the perfection they hoped to find
in solitude, still hearing Lenny Barker say
he likes those misty evenings—he gets a good grip
on the ball—hearing a distant cello driving through
Bach's perfect variations, each as shapely
as a nine-pitch inning, each one perfect,
each one bringing forth the next.

Fairport Carnival

In July, the carnival moves in;
streets down to the sand crack and rattle
as the Ferris Wheel rolls by, in pieces.
Her mother's voice circles the damp air
like a gull who watches for a movement
in the water. But she is walking, past
Hungarian and Finnish churches, past
the lighthouse to the sand where the carnival
is setting out temptations, and hot oil
for the star-shaped waffles, flecked with sugar.
She's walking on the breakwater, its huge rocks
hot on her bare feet; she's waiting for
a gypsy who will bring his horse. She'll feed it
chunks of apple, loving the grating tongue
across her palm; she'll break hot waffles
and bring his fingers to her mouth, still smeared
with sugar. He'll teach her how to trust
the horse's back and his encircling arms
as they canter so far west along the shore
they can't see the tiny midway lights;
she'll coax him through the waves and teach him
how to give his body to the water.

The Loudest Woman in Lake Erie

Water pebbles, smooth as teeth, cloudy as a gull's eye,
clink and rattle in the wave's lap while the loudest woman in
   the lake
hauls the morning up with a whoop, shaming the roosters.
She yells the whitecaps flat,
her howls foghorn across the bottom, box the watery ears
of sailors, unlucky passengers; her songs shriek the bones
up from the sand and fishtails scrape like fiddle bows
while she calls a square dance for the drowned.

She can send storms whimpering back west
but it's the small noises she can't bear:
waves soughing up and back, wind combing the shore poplars,
because towns of sailors' wives wait there. They stare
to the blank horizon, waiting for smoke, a sail,
some blotch on the pure arch of the lake's spine
while sand crawls into their hems.
The loud woman weeps to see them, howls at the skyline
that each day lies flat and clean.

At night she hides from the lighthouse's long eye,
but it slaps her skull, grates through its long ride
like a millstone chewing glass.
The women bend to her, cry for an end to watching
and she runs north to drag the winter down
so the waves will stop
and they will hear nothing but wind twisting the bare poplars

while the lake stands up, frozen,
like a horse surprised in the middle of a plunge.

The poplars and the women sleep;
snow ripples on the sand while the loudest woman in the lake
stares to the frozen waves
warm in the quiet that spreads wide as the Northern lights,
long and clean as ice.

- COOK FOR PEOPLE IN SC
- GO SOMEWHERE W/ DR. IN COLA
- TRAUMA TRIGGERS

E

NEG BELIEF → REPROCESS
TRIGGERS
SHRINK NEG. BELIEF

EMDR

BIO STIMULATION

- GROUNDING
- 5 SENSES

COPING SKILLS
BODY MAP

—

10AM
FRIDAY 12/9/22

- GINGER
- PEPPERMINT

} SHUT DOWN / DEEP BREATHS

- COPING SKILLS FOR ZONES

MEDITATE — HIKING RIDGE (MARCH)

ITAINAR FOR SPACE | ACORN

SPICES: • CRUSHED RED PEPPER
• CHOLULA • FRANK'S RED HOT •

ORGANIZATION : • SHOE RACK • STORAGE
FOR DVDS/BLU RAYS •

T 215
69
275

West to Ohio

It has been very cold & dusty riding today—We have met with no adventure yet, of any kind—We are now waiting at the ferry house to cross the river as soon as wind & tide serve—The white waves foam terribly how we shall get across I know not, but I am in great fear—If we drown there will be an end of my journal—

A Journey to Ohio in 1810
Margaret Van Horn Dwight

Getting Through the Winter:
Lake County, 1815

Meat and Corn

In Willoughby, the Widow Miller stitched up
homespun sacks for the corn she'd raised.
In town, she traded corn for salt to cure
raccoons she'd trapped, bagging the sharp chunks
of salt, each one more precious than the watery
pearls, pulled from rough blue mussels, that lay glowing
in the merchant's palm. Once, when a bear
surprised her in the corn, she whirled, grabbed the ax
that glittered in the sun, sharp as the bear's
black, determined, uncomprehending eyes.
After she had saved her life, she skinned
and salted him, and lived to be 100.

Their Next Meal

Joseph Talcott brought his family from Connecticut,
each lugging prayers and seed corn that they planted
in the same holes, hoping that the prayers
would warm the seeds against the April frost,
keep them from rotting in the mud which stayed
until the drought. That autumn, they had corn,
but no way to grind it when their stomachs
begged for mush and hoecake, so Joseph walked
from Madison to Cleveland, forty miles,
with forty pounds of corn roped in a sack
bulging with lumps and angles—as if he'd bagged
his children's knees and elbows. Three nights later,
he returned, with a smooth sack of meal;

his wife cooked mush at midnight, and woke the children
who had gone to bed with hunger wrapping
their thin bones like a poultice.

Walking Through the Country

Ebenezer Merry came on foot, carrying his faith
that wilderness would feed him if he worked his body
down to soul and sinew, against fire and the Black Swamp,
that vestige of the ancient lake, where the forest floor
was marsh and trees blocked the sun. Each night,
    he greased his only
pair of boots with fat from the last animal the forest
gave him, and woke once to find the boots chewed to the soles
by a wolf or fox who never let a meal escape. By autumn,
he could thresh chestnuts from their burrs with his bare foot.

Taking Ice

In Fairport Harbor, they stored the winter
against summer. When fields froze, when the lake
refused to give more than thumb-sized fish, ice
was their only crop. Horses dragged blades across
the ice, stumbling where a wave had left its shape,
marking lines for men who walked behind
with ax and saw. They cut blocks as wide and long
as the ice was deep; they cut a channel
so the men with pikes could pole the perfect squares
up to the ice house where they stored their harvest,
cheap as air, precious as meat, as dangerous
to bring in as fish from the wild center
of the lake, or salt from the fragile tunnels
under the mutable uncharted water.

Coming into the Country

1. 1827

A ship left from Liverpool, well stocked
with English families who had been promised
that Ohio was a green and pleasant land.
Three weeks out, a small girl died and was sewn
into a scrap of canvas, folded square
across her cold face as neatly as the caps
her mother stitched. In the ship's log, her father
wrote, "Our Isabella was committed
to the deep and was seen no more."
The white parcel was pushed gently from the stern
and vanished without a splash or murmur;
snowflakes fell on the enclosing water all that night.

2. June, 1850

The steamer G.P. Griffith loaded up
 a hundred Germans and more Irish,
bound west from Buffalo. When the fire started,
just off Fairport Harbor, it burned the lifeboats
first; they fell, black and hissing, to the warm water.
The passengers jumped off; the lake raised no waves,
but did no more than usual to hold them up.
A few Irish got to shore; the Germans sank
because they wore their slender fortunes sewn
in linen belts. When the lake gave up
their bodies, they were laid in trenches where
the sand gives way to soil; years later,
the lake pushed into their graves and took back
whatever of the New World they'd purchased.

3. 1860

Before the war, slaves came to the county
hidden in wagons, or wrapped in darkness,

following stars, and ax marks on the trees.
When they got to Painesville, or Fairport Harbor,
they found a few who kept secret chambers
on the lip of freedom—the Fairport lighthouse
keeper, or the hardware merchant whose pillared
mansion opened into tunnels on the river
where boats with muffled oars would wait.
When slave catchers, riding from Kentucky,
appeared in town, the merchant built a mound
of hay bales in his wagon and drove
around with a dozen hidden slaves who tried
to smell the cold green river that would lead them
to the lake and the cold green of Canada.
He chatted with the owner of the *Telegraph*,
who hid slaves on his farm, who paid his workers
by printing notices of runaways.

4. Following the Prophet

When the Mormon prophet came to Kirtland,
he brought words of fire and gold that lured young
Peter from the Methodists to the river,
where he paced the bank and watched for something
shining through the golden aspens. Once he saw
an angel, black as a starless night,
holding a scrap of white that Peter knew
to be a letter sent from Heaven
to Ohio. He called; the angel's
midnight wings glowed upon the river's
face; he waded out to catch the letter
that would tell him where in all Ohio

50

he could feel his soul glow golden
as the aspens, all year long. He watched
the angel graze the treetops, blue-black
as a grackle, while the message caught
like a wet leaf at the river's distant
edge and sank in the swift water.

When the Unimaginable
Becomes Easy

After photography became popular, studios had an
abundance of glass negatives. They were often sold for
windows, both for homes and for greenhouses.

After the first photographers persuaded sunlight
to trace the things it saw on thick glass negatives;
when we no longer found ourselves amazed at seeing

unfading faces of the dead on mantelpieces;
when all America had posed, when every studio
had stacks of negatives left over,

then, south of the lake, nurserymen were digging rose fields,
building the wide greenhouses. They bought those stacks
of glass and fit them, side by side, in the fragile roofs

so that the seedlings—roses, onions, cabbages—could grow
beneath the solemn faces of the babies, some gowned
for christening, some dead but neatly dressed, their starched

white dresses blackened in the negative's reversal.
Soldiers, too, gazed on the new blooms, their coats and rifles
turned to cream and silver, their faces dark as smoke and dust.

Years of rose slips rooted while sunlight faded images,
their lines as faint as veins in last year's unnumbered leaves.
Fields of roses find their true form and color

under the sun that fades the unimaginable
numbers—twenty thousand at Antietam, thousands more
at Shiloh—in fields returned to pasture, wheat, or corn.

City Life

Gleaning

Early morning: trucks like iron ships on the expressway,
tanks brimming with the fuel of their destruction,
trailers stacked with crates of chickens, melons, apples—
dinner for each town they pass. These days,
it's no surprise to see a trailer overturned, its cargo
spilled into the waves of heat that lap the highway,
the concrete sticky with smashed eggs, smoking as the
    spilled
beef burns. It's too late now for the woman on the bus
to catch those eggs, or hook a chunk of beef—
each night she could trim charred fat and slice a meal.
The empty truck floats off through angry traffic;
snowplows scrape the bounty to the shoulders, a feast
for flies and rats, too late to carry out Jehovah's
law: after harvest, all the scattered bounty
that the scythes and knives passed over must be left.
And the fatherless, the stranger, and the widow
must be allowed to come to the stripped fields to fill
their baskets with barley, grapes and olives before
the sun and soil, who need nothing, claim it as their own.

Spare Change

Crossing Spruce Street, I was bending like a peddler
under my laundry and three loaves of day-old bread.
She held her sleeping daughter, asked for change for milk,
and diapers to soak up what the baby couldn't use.
I'd spent my change on laundry tokens, flat imitations
rattling in my hand. I offered bread; she needed cash;
we stared at the broken street, as if we hoped to see
a table spread with laundered white, with knives and baskets
ready for the strong bread that, broken open,
would release a blessing in the smell of yeast.

Feeding Demons

(Mark 5:1)

I'm sawing, puzzled, at a raw pork shoulder,
unused to meat so like the chunk of beast
it came from, skin thick as moccasins
binding half an inch of fat. Rosemary
and garlic won't make it edible
or pretty; all I can do is spread
its savor into two pounds of beans,
wishing that by feeding guests and family
I could erase the gaze of fury
from the man who asked for change
as I struggled with my grocery bags.

Once, a man crazed by unclean spirits cried
"What have I to do with thee, Oh Son of God?"
As Jesus drew the demons out, they pleaded
to be sent into the herd of swine
grazing on the mountain. Two thousand pigs
tore downhill to the sea and choked
on the salt, unfriendly water.

Imagine our city's hungry, crowding
grocery doors, sending their stomachs' devils
into our brown bags. Imagine bread
and apples full of spirits mad from hunger,
racing through our bodies; imagine
how we'd chase those hungry men and women
through the littered streets, begging them to bless us,
free us from the gnawing spirits
ravenous for our flesh.

Saving the Prophet

On Market Street, they're raising a new tower,
taller than the last, testing the willingness
of glass and steel to hold each other up.
A street man waves his sweaty Phillies cap—
WORLD CHAMPIONS in gold stitching on the brim—
and warns the construction crew how their wide
glass wall catches the late sun, tosses it
against the glass tower across the street
where it swells, bouncing between the walls
like a newborn star, until glass and steel
could vanish in a gush of flame.

They listen to him, split their sandwiches
and one sips gently from his bottle.
That evening as they close the site, they find him
sleeping, six copies of the *Daily News*
under his head. They circle him with plastic
safety cones, hoping that police and dogs
will hear the fluorescent orange calling *let him sleep;*
they lay his cap across his eyes to shield him
from the orange sodium glare of streetlights
burning like the city's anger, lingering
in the smoky air past dawn.

City Music

High-Heeled Sneakers

Half-past five: I'm striding home in sneakers
when I overtake the best-dressed woman on the block
moving grandly over shards of ice in high-
heeled pumps that match her purse. I want to tell her
how all Market Street—the brogues, aerobics, clogs,
galoshes—all kick their shabby heels and cheer
because she struts on plastic legs, hollow
from the knees on down, clipped on each morning
like a bow tie, and slipped into her glossy shoes.

I'd like to follow as her polished slippers
dare the ice to trip her, clumping up four flights
to rooms where music flows across the waxy
floors when we march in. She opens frivolous
pink wine, fills goblets thin as the evening ice-skin
on the concrete, tells how, if I learn
to dance with her, I'll learn the body's flawed
and partial wisdom that turns fashion
into grace. The screws at her knee joints squeak;
I kick off my clumsy shoes and bow to her.

Heart and Soul

It's February; sparrows are announcing
that I've filled the feeders; my daughter's crying
because the paper hearts she's cut are crooked
and kids in the row houses cheek by jowl with ours
are banging "Heart and Soul" on their pianos.
My daughter joins them; just last week, she learned it
from the right-hand neighbor who'd learned it from
the left-hand kid. Its jaunty bass line bounces
through our common walls, a message between children
who used to cry at night, but who now tell stories

to explain the strange protrusions on their parents'
bodies, their twittering as foreign to us
as the signals between hungry birds.
No piano teacher plays that song;
it's for children who believe that heart and soul
and body are all one, who know that they can run
on railroad tracks, can leap from piers into unmeasured
water, can love the wiry bodies which will soon
betray them. But for now, heart, soul and flesh
are wound together, wrapped and stitched as tightly
as a baseball which they could throw
in a perfect arc, out of our fumbling reach,
far from our fading voices calling them home, once more.

Lightly Row

Six a.m. October; dawn has grown so awkward
that some days we can't believe the sun has had
a billion years of practice lighting up the ragged
sycamores. Our neighbor's warming up his cello:
a few long yearning notes, the patient scales,
the simple melodies, "Bagatelle" and "Lightly Row."
At forty, he began to study what he'd loved,
to fill the second half of life with songs whose
repetitions, calming as the stroke of oars
on unresisting water, pass through his thrumming
strings to soothe the petulant street noise, the nervous
humming of the heart that each day practices
its ending. Though common sense said no,
it isn't worth the trouble, he remembered the stubborn
woman who at eighty began to study
Hebrew so she could "greet God in his own language."

Daily News

When we rented the one-bedroom up on Baring Street
the landlord coughed—it wasn't empty, his dead tenant
had left some papers in the living room. We imagined
a few cartons full, then gasped to see the room stacked, floor
to ceiling, door to door, with *Inquirers,* even
Bulletins, bound with twine, piled like bricks or lumber
as if he'd hoped to build a room to hide in, or walls
to block the squeal of buses that couldn't take him
far enough, of police cars that could rescue anyone
but him. The landlord shrugged; he'd known a dozen
stackers, each one a nuisance. I'd seen that tenant once,
silent, gray as newsprint. He played the radio all night,
some station without English, full of gutturals
and sighs. Why did he save those papers? Did he plan
to clip the day's worst stories and hand them out to us
like tracts, first weeping for the blameless dead, like those
who mourned in Bethlehem when Herod slew the children,
then calling glory, glory, how blessed we are to have escaped
that day's fire and sword? Would we thank him?

Who Knows

In every neighborhood there's one who sees and knows;
we have one who knows more than she tells, more
    than we'd wish.
She knows who ought to leave, who cries at breakfast—
all that silent, terrible love that starts at home.
When they finally found the missing woman, three years dead,
she said she'd known it all along; the man, she said,
let anger run into his fists, the woman couldn't
listen to her fear which told her *leave, and don't come back,*
fear which crackled around her fragile shoes like leaves
from our exhausted trees. Those three years, our patient
neighbor watched the cats whose tails rose like signals
on his porch. Behind a wall so weak her cries, his shouts
would blow into the street like scraps of paper,
there was a locked trunk where her drying body lay,
folded like a coat he'd never wear again,
but couldn't give away. The cats would sniff the floor
but never told if what they smelled once stained his pants
and his clean, protesting fingers. This knowledge blows
around us, fresh as each day's paper, as constant
as the sycamores and our neighbor's vigil,
sitting on her step until it rains and the cats
go where they can. All this settles in her like the cat
hair drifting behind her chair, months after her last
cat died. He was ugly, cross, and cried at night;
she cooked him liver and let him sleep beside her,
but he had leukemia and she dare not
get another for five years, at least.

Watching the Movies

Hollywood's been camping on our quiet street, aiming false
daylight into the rented house they've stripped and dressed
so we won't know it. We stare behind their chalk lines,
waiting while the experts on the actors' perfect bodies
comb and zip and preen; the director waits for bus and clouds
to pass, as patient as the wise general who, freezing in his torn
tent, remarked that war is mostly waiting.

We're waiting for our neighbor to be set in motion—
the only one they've rented from our street. He's been groomed
and rouged, buttoned in a suit, and stands as unprotesting
as he did in Vietnam where he never saw the enemy,
though one night his platoon was camped above a buried
village full of rooms, where the people he'd been trained
to shoot would wait for weeks, moving underground like water.

Since coming home, he's seen a thousand movies, and thinks
if he can watch himself up there, he'll see what's real
and what's a story, stitched together like the strips
of film that make a battle scene, or the jagged line
of jobs and door keys that he's walked along since then,
between the movies, with nothing holding it together
but his waiting for a cup of coffee, for a phone call,
for a voice that tells him you can sleep now, sleep.

Maintaining the Species

In the zoo's glass room, two dozen warblers
from New Guinea hop and preen. They're ten percent
of all surviving since the snakes, imported
to eat rats, swallowed birds instead. Here,
the birds are bred and counted, but no one
thinks they can return to their green island;
the snakes fill every tree and hollow.

Their keeper once believed, that with luck and time,
he could revive lost species, could take
the leathered pterodactyl from its peg
in the Museum and slowly breed
a new one. But now, too tired to be
a god, he waits for the warbler's eggs,
going sleepless while they hatch. He's rescued them;
he mourns their cages but knows he'd do the same
for snakes and rats; it's all his job, like a mother
grieving because her children bite and curse each other.

Earrings

He told her with his knife
to pull the hoops from her soft
scarred lobes and cross his angry
palm with the gold she'd worked
a hundred nights to buy, the wrought
metal that could pay her rent.
They gleamed against her braids

like the beads and coins chattering
on the dresses of village women
in the high green hills.
They wear their wealth, their bangles
clicking out *good woman,*
their earrings multiplying
sunlight while they wear their pride,
their pleasure undisturbed.

But he put his knife against
her earrings; as she still said no,
he took more than he wanted,
leaving her no coin to lay
on Charon's heavy palm,
leaving nothing for her friends
to weight her eyelids,
leaving her no chance to test
the difference between gold
and her young body, untouched
and unadorned.

No Expiration Date

my coupon says. Good forever? Like the light
perpetual that shines, so the Requiem says,
in Heaven? The Chinese feast on eggs they'd buried
months before; the *Enquirer* loves to show us women
who give birth from eggs that might be dried by now,
or spoiled. Could I limp into the Acme
in 2020 and claim my quarter off the price
of Cheerios? I could be stooping near the milk,
squinting at the cartons that still show children's faces.
If, each time I needed milk, I had to buy my daughter's
    face,
would waxy pictures, cut from a thousand cartons,
now fill my table? Would I keep her eyes and face,
repeated on those sour squares, hoping I could
take one to the grocery and redeem her unchanged
face and body? But no: each day the photographs
would grow more useless, so finally I would sit,
wishing that the milk could make me sleep
lest I end up like the Sybil who asked to live
forever, but forgot to ask for lasting youth,
and so she lived on, lonely, aching through her dusty
joints, cursing everything that keeps.

First Death

The cat was ill-behaved and old; his heart no longer pumped
with the stubborn force it needed to flush water from
his abdomen, so, when he swelled, bewildered by the sag
of flesh and fur between his legs, all they could do was let
the vet's efficient gases work. He came home in a towel,
to be buried near a garden bench, but first they had to tell
their daughter about death, again, then sing a song. "Baa baa
Black Sheep," she suggested, and when they'd sung, it began
to rain again, an unwelcome blessing after six wet days.
The moon came glowing out, pulling excess water
from this patch of earth, helping their tired hearts wring
water from their bodies, keeping the fresh bones shrouded
in the earth. They slept, thankful for the moon that keeps
floods in check, knowing if the moon fails, rain will wash
the cat's bones to their steps. The black sheep will see
the open door, and scratch and cry; he's naked to the bone
again, it's raining and they will take him in.

Child Care

I sometimes think I did my best for her
when I wrapped her like a hothouse bud
that mustn't freeze—bunting, blanket, blanket,
cap—and strapped her to my chest.
But now she's crying; there's a red lump behind
her ear and, quickly, all the sick children
I have known, or charmed into existence
in the heat of fear, stand in her bedroom,
faces chalked with the dust of suffering
like the kings who showed Macbeth his future.

Going to the doctor's, we pass a woman
driving down the street, left hand on the joy stick
of her electric wheelchair, right hand gripping
the thick strap that pulls her laughing daughter's
stroller, a sack of diapers hanging from the back.
She brakes and turns, the child's wheels curving
inches from the parked cars, in measured safety,
as if some blue-shirted angel follows,
whistling like a traffic cop, arms waving
tender semaphores as she drives past.

Double Dutch

My first week in the city, I watched in awe—
girls not five feet tall, twirling two ropes at once
while the third rushed in, slipping her slim legs
between the ropes that braided the compliant air,
that hissed like snakes eager to trip her up,
to cover her graceful legs with bruise and scar.

The ropes revolved in patterns like the sine
and cosine curves I loved in high school.
I barely understood them, but traced their arcs
as if they could lift me up and set me down,
moving outward on the axis toward
a point that glitters like an unnamed planet.

Now, my daughter envies older girls
jumping in the school yard, ropes tossing the air
in waves, their hair streaming in the breezes
of their joy like the carved locks of figureheads
that breast the waves, moving out from shore
where I am learning not to say *come back*.

Combing Out the Tangles

Her hair winds about my brush like thread
upon a spindle, thread that turns to gold
at the sun's first transforming word as if
some joking fairy let me spin her beauty
without telling me the price. I spin all night:
she'll grow more lovely and quickly leave.

Tangling in the wind of her excitement,
her hair has turned upon itself in tiny
knots; she pulls away as if my comb
bites into a nest of spiders whose bright
webs, pressed on wounds, can heal without a scar.

She'll never let me brush her hair again
or wash the whorls and creases of her body.
She's left us holding our useless combs.
At the mirror, she caresses her bright hair
with all its tangles, tough as the chrysalis
that hides the golden moth.

Seeking the Buddha

I braid her soft hair, then watch her loping
through the school yard. Perhaps one day in ten
I think *This could be the last time,* not even
thinking of the California school yard
and his nameless rage and the long rifle
ordered from a magazine, not thinking
of the school yard where a car climbed steps
and unlocked gates at lunchtime, on a sunny day—
just thinking all it takes is the magnetic
love between a bike and swerving car and that
could be the last time.

There's a story of a woman who would wear
her dead son everywhere, sprawling on her back
like a sleeping infant or a sack of rice.
The village wise man stopped her at the well:
"Seek the Buddha's help" and she walked—how many
miles?—with her dead son—how heavy?—on her back.
The Buddha, sorrowful, told her he would make
a medicine to cure the boy, but only
if she brought him mustard seeds from a house
where death had never visited. She set off,
then returned with empty hands and pockets,
holding the blue jacket that her son had worn,
planning to fold it on his pillow
or hang it like a spring kite on the wall.

School Fire

Our Lady of the Angels
Chicago, December 1, 1958

The brass doorknob could still sear his skin
when the fireman plunged his fire ax through the lock
to see two dozen children, books and lunch pails
balanced by their feet, hands folded, heads down
as if the principal had rustled in
to bless them. The school had bowed for the day's
last prayer when the fire climbed stairs, burst from windows
with a shout before anyone could say
Amen, or Fire, or Run. On the playground,
mothers waited for the bell; gulls, which some
children thought were angels, fled mewing
to the frozen lake, frightened by sirens
and the father who passed thirty children
into his neighbor's arms and found his daughter
searching for her pencils and her red shoe.
In the crowd, wimples rose and bent like gulls;
upstairs, a sister soothed her class with prayer
and they fell asleep, while pure heat, stripped
of its light, knocked her into the chalky wings
of the Holy Ghost, brooding on the blackboard.
Her starched guimpe crackled as the smoke pulled
her down and breathed into her mouth.
If angels wept around her puckering scalp,
the children could not hear them. They slumped, mouths
stopped in the shape of cries; flames blotched their folded
hands like the wings of four and twenty blackbirds.
They could not see the fire undress her slowly;
she fell asleep with fire as her true spouse
and angels as the soft bursts of ash
hanging on her lashes.

Playing with Fire

My first grade teacher, born in 1900,
read us the cautionary tales she'd learned;
thus we heard of Little Kettlehead
who played with matches, burned her hair and skull
and had to wear a bright tin pot inverted
on her stumpy neck. Her grieving parents
tied bright bonnets where her chin should be
and listened for her scarred voice—"I'm sorry
to have disobeyed"—rasping in her tin cave
of error and repentance.

In Hiroshima, those who lost their hair
hid their clean bare skulls with blue scarves, printed
white with cranes lifting their wide wings over
the seven-branched river. Those who survived
the flash of light ran into that river
until the water was so full of people
that the first ones there were pushed out to drown.
Cranes, it is believed, have healing powers,
but can they erase the scars from those
who could not shield themselves? And can the breeze
from their huge wings disperse the laughter
of those who live unscarred? They mock the burned
lips and skulls that pass so quietly;
they cry *bald ones, hairless monkeys, kettleheads,*
curses, charms against a third coming
of the planes whose silver bellies opened
over the city, just starting out for work.

Anna and the Steel Mill
is the 1995 First-Book Winner in the
TTUP Poetry Award Series.